HISTORIC PICTURES OF

BOURNE

LINCOLNSHIRE

compiled by

Michael McGregor

Market Place, Bourne

Contents

<u>South Aisle Memorial Window</u> of 1911, to Reverend Mansfield, Vicar from 1881-1910. The Abbey church is dedicated to St. Peter and St. Paul. The importance of St Peters Pool to the origins of the town is echoed in the need of a spiritual fountain head - "Ho everyone/ that thirsteth / come ye / to the water," as on the shield in the centre pane. The shield at the bottom left is that of the Wake family on which the town arms were based.

<u>Coat of Arms of Bourne U.D.C.</u>
granted 23 July, 1953.

This was based on the arms of the Wake Family, medieval lords of the manor, who lived in Bourne castle. The three discs remain at the top, but the two transverse bars are replaced by a wavy band on a single bar, to represent the Bourne Eau and Car Dyke, and the Hereward Knot to represent the son of Bourne who resisted William the Conqueror

The closed helm and mantling above is the emblem of a civic authority. The ermine lion rising from the battlemented tower represents the Cecil family, of Burghley House, who succeded as Lords of the Castle Manor. The Lion holds a shield with Fleur-de-Lys from the arms of the Digby family of the Red Hall.

The motto below, "Watch and Pray", is no bad advice to citizens dealing with a local authority.

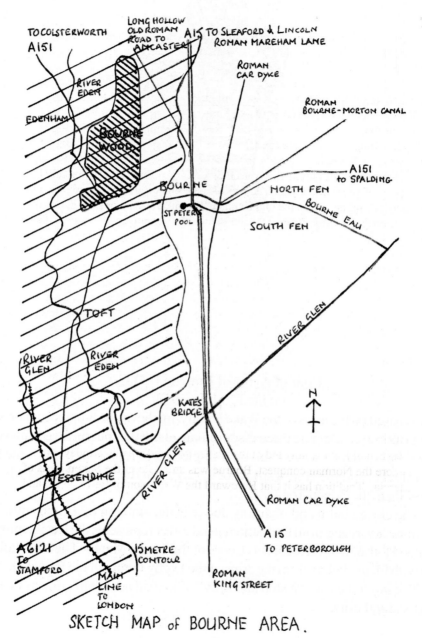

SKETCH MAP of BOURNE AREA.

4

Introduction and Early History

A growing old market town of some 11,000 population today, Bourne is 16 miles north of Peterborough on the A15 route to Lincoln, where it is crossed by the A151 to Spalding.

In ancient times this was the east coast track, between the wooded upland of the limestone ridge to the west, and the 35 mile wide stretch of fen, tidal flats and estuary to the east. Once, Bourne Fen too was wooded, as shown by the many "bog oaks" turned up by deep ploughing in the shrinking peat soil. Alongside this fen edge route were natural springs now embanked in St. Peter's Pool, the source of the Bourne Eau, which runs a tamed course three miles east to join the River Glen at Tongue End. It was this reliable supply of pure water which led to the settlement around its source and gave it its name. From the Old English "Burna" a stream or spring, like the northern burn, came Brunne, hence Brunnians for natives of the town, then Bourn. The e was added at the railway company's request in 1894, to avoid confusion with Bourn in Cambridgeshire.

In Roman times this track became the military King Street, dividing just north of Meadowgate into Mareham Lane, continuing to Sleaford and Long Hollow Way going north-west to join Ermine Street at Ancaster. On the fen edge, the Romans dug the Bourne-Morton canal, north-east towards a navigable inlet of the Wash, now disappeared, and the Car Dyke. This was a 76 mile dike from Peterborough nearly uninterrupted, almost as far as Lincoln. Its prime function was to act as a catchwater to avoid freshwater inundation of the fen from the higher ground to the west, and it still serves this function but it also acted as the western boundary of a Roman imperial estate in the fen. The fen was a very rich source of fish, wildfowl, peat fuel and reeds for thatching and flooring. Drainage for pasture was piecemeal at the edges, until the concerted efforts of the wealthy "adventurers" in the 17th century, eventually led to the rich arable land we know today.

Before the Norman conquest, Bourne was an estate of the Saxon Earls of Mercia. Tradition has it that Hereward the Wake, son of Earl Leofric and Lady Godiva, of the legendary ride in Coventry, was born in their manor house here. He is famed as one of the last Saxons to resist the Conqueror from his hideout in the fens nearby. Later, he made his peace with William I and in the Domesday Survey of 1086 is recorded as holding lands in Barholm, Witham on the Hill, Toft, Manthorpe and Rippingale, while Oger the Breton held the Manor of Bourne. The name Wake is not recorded until 1166 when Hugh Wake became lord of the manor on his marriage to the daughter of Baldwin fitzGilbert de Clare.

5

It was this Baldwin who built Bourne Castle and founded in 1138, the Augustinian Abbey, endowing it with land and dues from churches, parishes and mills. Thus Bourne came to have two manors, that of the castle, the manor of Bourne and that of the Abbey, the manor of Bourne Abbots. Both were served by the northerly diversions of the Eau, with their own fish ponds and mills. The Abbey had two fish ponds in the east. One became the open air swimming pool in 1922. The other was filled in for the Sleaford railway line in 1872. Its flour mill still further east in Victoria Place, became Notley's overshot mill but was demolished in 1973 for housing.

The castle was of the motte and bailey type, initially wooden but later with a stone keep on the large artificial mound and stone gate-houses. The main defences were palisaded banks and a complex system of moats fed by the diverted Eau and a shallow lake with horn-work to the south. The area within its extreme perimeter approached 20 hectares. There are signs of fish-rearing tanks to the west of St.Peter's Pool and its mill was to the east, on the site of the breast shot Baldock's Mill in South Street, now the Heritage Centre.

The castle's manor of Bourne again passed by marriage to the Cecil family in the early 16th century. In 1520, William Cecil was born in the manor house in the Market Place, the site of the Burghley Arms. He became Chief Secretary of State and Lord High Treasurer to Queen Elizabeth I, and built Burghley House near Stamford. By his death in 1598, the castle had been in decline for some 220 years and was largely ruinous. So, when we have the last report of it being garrisoned, on 11th October 1645, it will have been a Parliamentary response to a threatened raid on the town, mounting artillery on earthworks. The stone of the castle was used in much building in the town as at Wellhead Cottage and the Shippon Barn. Only a small portion of the motte remains, with depressions and ridges in the Wellhead Field, but the Eau still flows round the northerly edge. Behind Mr. Cliffe's shop in West Street is a mill wheel pit of eighteenth century brick, the remains of a small mill apparently once used for crushing bark for tanning.

There were several fires in the town in the 17th century. One, in 1605, lasted three days and led James I to make an official appeal for help. In 1637, the Eastgate area suffered severely. This may have contributed to the demise of the pottery industry there. It was still the commercial area of the town with wharves alongside the Eau for the import of bulk cargo like stone or coal and, no doubt, the export of wool or grain by way of the River Glen and coastal shipping in the Wash. In 1781 there was a Bourne Navigation Act to re-dredge the Eau but the coming of the railway in 1860 ended boat traffic. However, increased rail, then road traffic did help the town centre prosper, in meeting the needs of the agricultural district around.

The 1860s also saw the development of photography. By the turn of the century, there was a vogue for sending postcard views. It only cost a halfpenny, so most of the pictures we have are from the first decade of the 20th century and feature places on the map of 1909. They show us Victorian and Edwardian Bourne through the eyes of local photographers, notably Redshaw of North Street and Ashby Swift of South, then West Street. Most are unattributed and undated, so I have chosen to order them topographically rather than chronologically, including where possible, dates and additional information, which I hope, will add to their intrinsic interest.

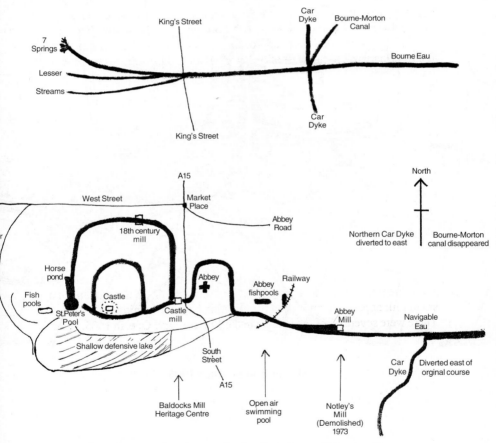

Sketch map showing northerly diversions of Bourne Eau
To defend the castle and service the Abbey

7

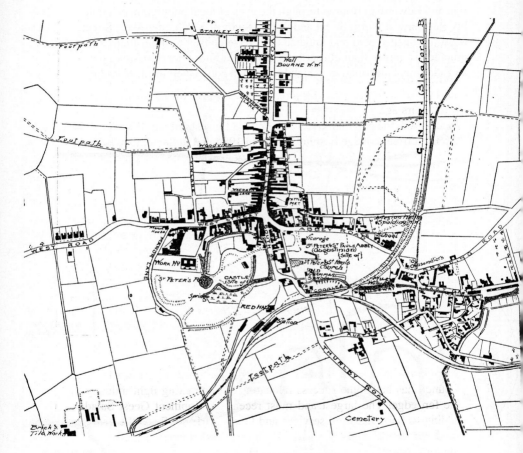

Map of Bourne dated 1906

Map of Bourne 1906

The two big changes in the Map of Bourne have been the growth of housing and the disappearance of the railways. Pre- and post-war, the Urban District Council (U.D.C.) steadily increased council housing, chiefly in the inner Northeast quadrant, but with the development of Peterborough in the 1960s, an explosion of private house building has covered virtually all the fields on this map. There are few houses east of the Car Dyke or in the Southwest quadrant but this is being developed now. To the west housing extends to Bourne Wood and northwest new building has covered the route of the officially proposed bypass, earmarked on the maps of forty years ago.

Since 1960, the population has doubled but the last rail was lifted in 1964, the Butterfield cottage hospital closed in 1984 and in September 1998 the Bourne Hospital on South Road was closed. Our two medical practices and the schools have been enlarged repeatedly. The Abbey Road primary school is on the 1906 map as it was the Star Lane Board School of 1877. The tiny Grammar School in the churchyard, endowed in 1636 by William Trollope was closed in 1903. The present Grammar School just north of the cemetery in South Road opened in 1921, in two wooden ex-army huts from Belton Park, which were used as classrooms until 1992. The Secondary Modern School began in 1944 in the prefabricated buildings of the present Youth Centre in Queen's Road. This was developed later behind Edinburgh Crescent to become the Robert Manning School, now with indoor pool and leisure centre alongside. The Westfield Primary School was built in 1975 behind the Villas of West Road. The Willoughby Special Needs School was opened south of the Grammar School in 1980. The excellent reputation of all our schools is one factor which keeps Bourne growing.

To balance this residential development the South Kesteven District Council has had some success relocating and attracting light industry to the fen edge. The largest and most recent development Geest Salads , adding to Salveson food services and Geest Stirfry, reflects the growing food processing industry. Opico, Boothman and Nursery Supplies are in the longer tradition of agricultural trade. The more surprising association of Bourne with motor sport continues with Mike Pilbeam's racing cars designed and built on Graham Hill Way. They have won seventeen out of twenty recent hill climb championships. Other motor firms are Pat Carvath of Manning Road and John Sismey's Lahoma Engineering, designing and making parts for racing cars among others and Trans Tech making castings for the general motor trade.

However, a great attraction of Bourne must be the green belt of public space so close to the town centre acquired by the Bourne United Charities (BUC), largely due to the foresight of their clerk, Horace Stanton, and so well maintained for the townsfolk by their groundsmen. So it is with this area of the Wellhead fields and Memorial garden, between Manor Lane and South Street and the Abbey Lawn, between Church Walk and Victoria Place, that I shall begin.

The Red Hall sketched in 1846 by J. Mills of Mills and Baxter, West Street. Built about 1600, lived in by the Fisher then Digby families, in 1859 it was sold to the Bourne and Essendine Railway Company. Although losing its sylvan setting and walled garden, it is amazing that it still stands, despite up to fifty trains a day rattling by so close for a century. Largely due to the persistance of Councillor Jack Burchnall it was aquired by the B.U.C. in 1962, restored and opened in 1972 to provide facilities for the community and the Charities.

1.	Looking at the <u>Wellhead field</u>, SW of St Peter's Pool, source of the Eau. A rare picture, being precisly dated and captioned as "The second battalion of the Lincs Regt. encamped in the trenches at Bourne 1 Sep 1897". No doubt here to parade in the celebrations for Queen Victoria's 60th Jubilee celebrations.

2.	<u>St. Peter's Pool</u>, a constant source of pure water, until recent dry summers and increased water extraction lowering the water table has meant the natural springs have dried up at times. Normal flow was 4.5 mill. gallons/day. Behind is the workhouse for some 300 paupers, opened in 1837, when Queen Victoria came to the throne. In 1939, it became St. Peters hospital for long stay mentally subnormal patients of all ages. It closed in 1994, and has been bought by Warners (Midlands) Ltd. to extend their magazine printing works from the adjacent old maltings.

(Ashby Swift)

3.   The <u>Bourne United Provident Association,</u> established in 1837, was a mutual self help group, funded by members' weekly subscriptions to provide finances to meet medical bills, sickness benefits and funeral costs. The officers met monthly in the Nags Head. The fund was gradually run down after the coming of the welfare state, but not finally wound up until 1994.

(posted 4th Oct.1911)

4.   Looking southeast from <u>the bridge over the Eau</u> where it leaves St. Peter's Pool (R) and becomes the horse pond (L). In the background (L) is the Wellhead cottage and Abbey church and (R) the mound of the castle motte in front of the trees, with the Red Hall and Station warehouse behind.

(published 1909)

5.   Looking south over the <u>Horse Pond</u> to St. Peter's Pool, with the workhouse grounds, widened in the late 19th century to increase the water reserve of the West Street mill, over the hedge (R). This is the first part of the Eau, diverted north to form the outer moat of the castle but now piped in.

6.   Looking north to the slope leading fron the horse pond onto <u>St Peter's Road</u>. Horses would be led in to drink, with carts to wash and wooden wheels to swell within their iron tyres. Where the swans are, is now a bore to allow pumping from the limestone aquifer below, if the natural spring flow has dried up.

7. Another spring south east of St. Peter's Pool supplied clear flowing water, ideal for growing <u>cress</u>. Started here by Nathaniel Moody in 1896, then run by Spalding UDC, then by South Lincs. Water Board from 1964 until closed in 1974, it is now filled in. In its hey day some three tons per week of freshly picked cress went off daily to London. The station was behind the Red Hall (R). In the distance (L) is Cavalry House and the pedestrian gateway to the Red Hall. This was demolished in 1918 by Prisoners of War, to make way for Tucks garage on South Road.

An Ashby Swift photo, posted by Eddie Moody on 2nd April 1915, saying "Bad day Tues. Snowed up. No milk trains running till Thurs. Spalding train snowed up for two days." Imagine gathering watercress in such weather.

8. All that remains of the <u>Castle Motte</u>, with the Red Hall behind. The artificial mound would have been much higher, with at first a wooden then stone keep. In dry summers, you can see the marks on the ground of the circular retaining wall at its base and two square rooms, no doubt protecting the base of the steps up. Near the tree on the left scorch marks can appear, where excavations in 1861 revealed evidence for a drawbridge over the inner moat (D on picture 9)

14   (McG 8 Feb 1986)

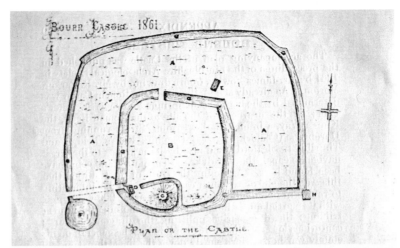

Bourn Castle. 1861

PLAN OF THE CASTLE

9. <u>Plan of the castle moats</u> produced after the excavations of 1861. The Eau was diverted north from St Peter's Pool (F) to form the castle moat. Now piped in, at first, it flows openly behind St Peters Road and West street, under South street car park, then attractivly alongisde South street to Baldocks mill (H). Nowadays there is usually a greater flow from the pool overflow directly to the mill (H). Only the eastern part of the inner moat holds rather stagnant water stopping short of the Shippon Barn (E). However, the northen and western part of the inner moat can be seen as depressions in the park.

10. <u>The castle site</u> from the Church tower, looking west. In the foreground is South Street, with Baldock's mill and F.H. Sones rate collector and coal merchant's hut in front of the Eau. Baldocks paddock behind, was the east bailey between the outer and inner moats, which would have been deeper and wider with embankments and pallisades. Behind the trees is the greatly reduced motte and inner bailey which would have enclosed many buildings of wood and later stone. The Wellhead cottage (R) was built of castle stone in the 17th Century. In the distance, St. Peter's Pool with Workhouse (R) and cress beds (L). In the far distance, the tiny cottage in Manor lane, was the first isolation hospital.

(published 1909)

11. The only recognisable remains of the castle buildings above ground are the crossbow arrow slits, re used in the gable end of the <u>Shippon barn</u> (E on the plan on picture 9) This was a crew yard and abattoir. In 1977 the barn was leased by the BUC to the Scouts and Guides Premises Comittee and is still in use every weekday evening by one or more units.

(McG 11 October 83)

12. <u>Baldocks mill pond</u> looking E with the inner moat to the left, and F.H. Sones hut and hay stacks in Baldock's paddock behind. Across the Eau in S. Strret can be seen The Cedars (now Bourne Eau House) and the Abbey Church. The three storey mill is directly ahead with the two storey miller's cottage attached (L). These buildings were leased by the BUC to the Bourne Civic Society in 1980 to become Bourne Heritage Centre.

(Posted Oct 1904)

13. Baldock's paddock was bought by the BUC from Lord Exeter, Lord of the Manor of Bourne, in 1947 and became the Memorial gardens. This shows the dedication of the cenotaph on the 16th Spetember 1956. Brigadier Richards of the Lincs. Regt. is on the left, his elbow partly hiding the face of H.M.A Stanton, Clerk of the Charity Trustees. On the front row is Alderman Day, Chairman of BUDC, D. Reeson Clerk to the BUDC and Councillor Dr. G. Holloway.

(Stamford Mercury)

14. Looking north along the Eau in South Street from behind Baldock's mill. The last miller John Thomas (Jack) Baldock with his son Richard in a punt powered by a Morgan car engine! Richard was killed on his motorcycle on the Spalding road soon after this photograph of July 1937. His two uncles F&H Baldock were killed in WWI and are listed among the 97 on the Cenotaph. On the other side there are only 32 names from WWII. The hut on the right was used by John Francis for drying herbs for pills, formerly F.H.Sones, of picture 15.

17

(Photo 1937)

15. <u>Brook Lodge</u> with the Abbey Church (L) and the garden of the Cedars (R). The Eau is piped under South street from Baldock's mill to emerge in the garden of Brook Lodge, and flow north around the Abbey complex. Brook lodge was built as the vicarage in 1776 but at the end of the 19th century, bacame Dr. Gilpin's home and Surgery. Later came Dr Keogh, Dr Montieth, Dr Holloway and Dr McGregor. The tiny lean-to at the rear was the waiting room, with the surgery times by the door over the message box, where medicines and prescriptions where put out for collection. The practice moved to St. Gilbert's Road in 1971 and in 1998 to the Hereward practice building in Exeter Street.

(McG 3 March 1962)

16. <u>Dr. Gilpin and his nurse in Church Walk</u> before the days of number plates required by the Road Car Act of 1903. Dr. Gilpin and T.W. Mays of Eastgate House were the first two people in Bourne to own motor cars. This is possibly a Dion-Bouton.

18

17. <u>Abbey House in Church Walk</u> built for W.O.Pochin, who followed the Trollopes as Lord of the Manor of Bourne Abbots. Abbey House was pulled down to build a new vicarage in 1878. That vicarage is now The Cedars Residential Home, with a nursing wing attached.

18. <u>The Abbey House seen from the Abbey Lawn</u> looking west. In 1922 the site was laid down as a bowling green, then the present vicarage was built on it in 1986. A rescue dig by archaeologists the year before, revealed the foundations of Pochin's Abbey House overlying the western range of the Abbey Cloister.

19. <u>Preparing the Abbey bowling green</u> in 1922, on the site of the Abbey House and earlier cloisters. Most of the figures are on the site of the Refectory. Canon Grinter has his foot on his spade (R).

20. <u>Arial view of the Abbey bowling green</u> (centre) with the old vicarage (now Cedars residential home, L) and the Abbey church (R).

Between Church Walk and South Street are Wherry's two yards, for pea processing (L) and animal feeds (R). Extreme left is the Red Lion yard. Right is the original Cedars, a complex house with parts from every century from the 16th to the 20th, on the site of the Abbey Infirmary. In its garden in front of the Abbey Church is the huge cedar tree which blew down on the 3rd January 1976, hence the change of name to Bourne Eau House. Brook Lodge is extreme right.

The Eau runs south (L to R) on this side of South Street, then comes from Baldocks Mill to Brook Lodge underground to emerge this side of Church Walk running north (R to L). Piped beneath Church Walk it runs east on the northern boundary of the bowling green (site of the present vicarage) and crosses the old vicarage gardens.

20

21. Print of 1819 showing the <u>Abbey House against the north side of the Abbey Church.</u> Founded in 1138, it is thought that the north west tower was never built. Perhaps there was a delay due to the Plague, or Black Death, by which time the subsidence of the South West tower was obvious. Clearly the west front was meant to be symmetrical, but doors and windows have had to be filled in and the tower buttressed.

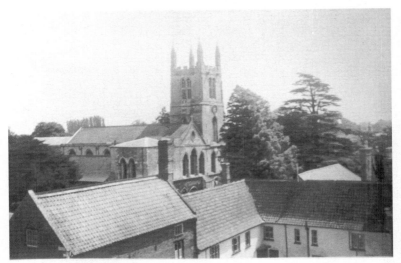

22. <u>The Abbey Church</u> from the roof of Wherry's warehouse on South Street, looking over the Cedars (now Bourne Eau House) with it's huge cedar tree in the garden. The west front was renovated by R.M. Mills (of Mills and Baxter, West Street) in 1883 when the large west window was replaced by three lancets in memory of his wife and two daughters, who died aged nine and under one year. This strengthened the support of the south west tower. It looks as if the north west tower was finally roofed in at a higher level than it appears on the print.

23. <u>The Abbey Church</u> tower obscured by the cedar tree as we look over the Eau and South Street, with The Cedars (L) and Brook Lodge (R). The garden railings, no doubt went to help the war effort in 1940.

24. The font at the <u>west end of the Abbey Church</u>, showing the box pews and twin aisles removed in the restoration of 1892, when the floor level was lowered.

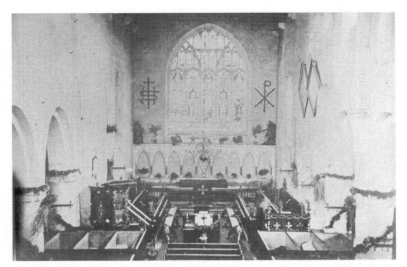

25 <u>Harvest Festival 13th Sept 1868</u>, showing box pews and the chancel floor level with the nave. The oak Jacobean pulpit was sold to the parish of Frampton, near Boston, for 3 guineas in 1890. The stone and marble arcading behind the altar was a gift of the Revd J. Dodsworth in 1866. The organ arch did not appear until later (see below).

26. <u>A later festival</u> showing the new pseudo Norman stone pulpit and lower nave floor with central aisle. One can see more clearly the brass chandelier of 1742, in memory of Mathew Clay's daughter who died aged 21. The nave arcades are the oldest part of the Abbey Church, with its massive pillars and Norman arches of the 12th century. The eagle lectern is of 1902.

posted June 1923.

27. <u>The Bourne Pageant in the garden of the old vicarage</u> (now Cedars residential home) in 1938, celebrating 800 years since the foundation of the Abbey by Baldwin fitzGilbert, Lord of the Manor. Thereafter there were two manors, that of the castle and that of the abbey, each with its own pond and watermill. The sites of Baldock's and Notley's respectively.

28. <u>The Eau flowing east through the Vicarage garden</u> and used in the historic pageant of 1938, here depicting the monks taking the body of Hereward "the Wake", to Crowland Abbey for burial. In the background we see across the bowling green to the wall on Church Walk, with The Cedars and Wherry's warehouse behind.

29. <u>The Abbey lawn from the church tower</u> showing part of Pochins sheep field already fenced off for football. To the right (S) of the Monks' Wall is the remaining monks' fish pond, which became the open air swimming pool and this side of it, the site of the grass tennis courts, the hut recently enlarged as the clubhouse. Beyond the pool and railway embankment is the pond of Notley's mill. In the middle distance the roof and chimney of the Gas Light and Coke company of 1840 at the head of Eastgate, to become the BRM works in 1960.

(posted 7th Nov 1950)

30. <u>The Abbey Lawn from the old Vicarage</u>, looking over the site of the new Cedars nursing home, and the hard tennis courts to the cricket and football pitches. Beyond the railway embankment is the gasholder on Spalding Road.

(McG 25th Aug 1962)

31. Mixed cricket on 8th Aug 1913. Bourne CC ahead of the MCC? This is the old pavilion burned down in 1963.

32. Bourne Town Football Team of 1924. Captained by Len Hird, butcher of West Street, who had won a military medal as a runner in the first World War.

33. The Swimming Pool, opened in 1922 and pictured here in 1923. Unheated with corrogated iron sides and a mud bottom, Dick Sellars says one could feel eels wriggling between the toes! No doubt they came in with the water which was run in from the adjacent Eau.

34. The pool in 1936 looking east towards the railway, with its signal over the fence. The four tier diving boards were installed in 1933. The pool was run by the BUC from 1932 until 1971, when the BUDC took over. A major improvement was the raising of money by the Round Table to instal heating in 1969. Fund raising is still vital, as the Council gave up running the pool in 1989 when they built the indoor pool in the Leisure Centre next to the Robert Manning School. Largely due to Councillor Mrs Patrick the Pool Preservation Trust was formed and is successfully running and improving this unique facility.

35. The Pool in the late 40s, looking west towards the Abbey Church, with the grass tennis courts between them. Just over the fence against the Monks' Wall is the little shed later enlarged as the tennis court clubhouse. Over the south fence (L) of the pool is the river Eau flowing east towards Notley's mill.

27

36. Labelled "Bourne Waterfall" on one postcard. I could not place this until I saw this picture labeled Coggles Causeway. It is the overspill from the mill pond behind Notley's Mill, showing the head of water available to turn the overshot mill wheel.

37. The river was held back to form Notley's Mill pond. This used to feeze over most winters and provide an excellent skating rink in the town. The head of the overspill is clearly seen in the foreground but only faintly in the distance to the west is the outline of Red Hall. The river is now piped in along the eastern half of Coggles Causeway.

38 <u>Notley's Mill in Victoria Place</u> beyond Queen's Bridge. This grain mill only ceased work shortly before demolition in 1972. On the left Branston's Dept. store, now Kinnsway Furnishers. The name Branston is still to be seen in the floor mosaic at each doorway.

(William Pearce)

39 <u>Queen's Bridge</u> over the Eau at the head of Eastgate, showing where they had provided a slope for horses and carts, as in St Peters Road (Picture 5). T Hinson's shop behind is now a house, with Rogers butchers shop built on the out house, obscuring the Independant Chapel, now United Reformed Church. Built by the Congregationalists in 1846, they were very well supported with 360-400 worshipers recorded in 1849 and some 150 in the Sunday School by the turn of the century, when the school room was built behind the church.

(Ashby Swift posted 1904)

40 <u>Cottages and Eastgate House</u> on the North Bank of the Eau just beyond the horse slipway. The cottages have gone but Eastgate House remains, the lifetime (1/8/99 to 6/1/80) home of Raymond Mays CBE. Better known as "RM", the motor racing ace who brought world wide fame to Bourne with pre war ERA and post war BRM cars, built in the works behind his home. At the extreme left of this picture is part of the gas showrooms now gone but the gas works behind were used to build BRMs .

41 <u>Raymond at the wheel of his first car</u> in Eastgate House yard. The details of this "mockup" were so good there must have been some some adult help. His father TW Mays fired Ray's interest in motorsport as he was an early car enthusiast, who took part in speed trials and hill climbs. Head of the family business of wool-stapling and fell-mongery, in Eastgate. TW Mays was also a JP, and in several years chairman of the Bourne UDC. He died in 1934, the year the first ERA car was completed.

(Posted 14th Oct 1908)

42 <u>Eastgate House yard in 1929</u> with "RM" in his Villiers Vauxhall Supercharge Special. Amhurst Villiers was at Oundle School, then Cambridge University with RM. A specialist at supercharging he lived at Eastgate House from 1922 - 25 working in the family business and on RM's cars. RM's Lagonda is in this garage, an Alpine Riley in front of the maltings and orchard greenhouse which were to become the ERA works.

43. <u>Eastgate House Yard during the 2nd World War</u>. The Bentley and three Rovers have blackout hoods on the headlights. The rear of the house is the oldest part with a well in the kitchen. Over the side door is the date 1796.

RM's mother, was one of three Shilcock sisters, whose father kept the Nag's Head in the Market Place. She was a staunch supporter, looking after RM and his resident collaborators and entertaining the many visitors from business, motor sport and show business. She was 97 when she died here in 1973.

44. <u>The two famous marques of racing cars built in Bourne</u>, seen in Rouen. Left, the pre war ERA of English Racing Automobiles, 17 were built between '34 and '39, most of which still race successfully today in VSC events. Right, the post war BRM of British Racing Motors, of the type that won the World Championship in 1962, with Graham Hill.

45. <u>Civic Reception in Bourne Corn Exchange</u> for the World Champion driver and Sir Alfred Owen, who saved the BRM project from financial ruin in 1952, by taking it into the Rubery Owen Organisation. He holds the scroll presented by the UDC. Behind (L to R) are his sister, Mrs. Stanley, RM, Graham Hill and Mrs. Tipler Chairman of the UDC. Successes in the '60s was followed by decline in the 70s and ultimate closure in 1980.

46. <u>The Anciens Pilots de Grand Prix</u> in the garden of Eastgate House on 17th July 1967. RM was very proud to be a member of this international club and invariably wore his blazer with their badge on the pocket.
Standing (L to R), Duncan Hamilton, R.M., Philipe Etancelin, Maurice Baumgartner, Juan Manuel Fangio. Down (L to R), Leslie Brooke, Louis Chiron, Stirling Moss and Emmanuel de Graffenried. Many other world famous drivers visited Eastgate House and drove ERAs or BRMs.

47. <u>The queue to view the last of the BRMs</u> on 11th Oct 1981 before they went for sale at Christies. Starting way down Eastgate they filed past Eastgate House and the old gas showroom, now gone, before turning into Willoughby Road and entering the old gas works yard.

48. <u>Washing skins on the north bank of the Eau</u>, outside the sheds of TW Mays "Lincolnshire's largest woolstaplers and fellmongers". Looking upstream towards the Anchor Inn. This was the head of the navigable Eau, which would allow the turning of boats.

(published 1908)

49. The path on the <u>east bank of the Car Dyke,</u> with Bedhouse Bank on the left, turns right to follow the Eau by the Anchor Inn. One of the roofs ahead must be the Butcher's Arms on Eastgate, which was demolished in May 1941 when a Junkers Ju 88 was shot down and crashed on it.

50. <u>Inside the skinning shed</u> where sheepskins where cleaned and sorted. It must have been unpleasant in hot weather having such a business close to the town. Note the gas lamp.

(published 1908)

51.<u>Delivering dead stock</u> for the other side of the business. It was the firm's boast as fellmongers that "every atom of the horses, sheep etc., reaching this works is turned to some commercial account". Thus the horse hair or wool was graded (stapled), the skins tanned, the flesh and bone turned to fertiliser and hooves and horn to glue.

(published 1908)

52. <u>Mays' lorries outside the fertiliser sheds in Cherry Holt Road</u>. These were First World War hangers brought from Norfolk and are still in use, although no longer for fertilisers.

53. <u>The mixing and bagging of fertiliser</u> within the shed. Later a granulation plant was built alongside for pelleting fertiliser, run by Albright and Wilson who took over T.W. Mays

54. <u>TW Mays annual root show in Hodgkinson's yard</u>, Abbey Road, was a publicity exercise to demonstrate how much better the crops were having used May's fertilisers. This was October 1914.

55. Aerial view of <u>Mays' boiling shop down the Slipe</u> in 1955. This was known as the "Bovril" factory from the pungent odours wafting over the town on an East wind. This is where the hooves and horns were turned to glue.

Chapter 2: Bourne waters, markets and Market Place

The previous chapter was loosely based on the river Eau and how it helped shape the development of the town. This chapter is intended to reflect something of the importance of Bourne as a trading centre for the district around, and the artesian water as a trading commodity.

The right to a weekly general market held at the crossroads by the north gate of the castle was granted to the Wakes as Lords of the Manor in 1299. Later inherited by the Cecils of Burghley house. Over the years up to four seperate annual fairs were granted to the town, chiefly for the trade in cattle and sheep. In late Victorian times, when our photography began, there were permanent pens in the cattle market behind The Bull and behind the Marquis of Granby in Abbey Road and occasional temporary sheep pens in West Street and the central Market Place. The weekly cattle market declined in the 1980s and the site has been cleared to become Budgen's car park. Around the cattle market were several agricultural firms, Friends', Holliday and Rickard's which have gone but there is still Johnson Brothers agricultural machinery in Manning Road. Alongside the market the Corn Exchange was built in Abbey Road in 1870. It is now a most valuable social centre for plays, organ recitals, concerts, dances, bazaars and receptions.

The central Market Place is dominated by the Town Hall built in 1821, with magistrates court "up the steps" and the market shambles below, part of which housed the town fire engine from 1900. The architect was Bryan Browning designer of the House of Correction at Folkingham. In recent years it has been cleaned outside, tastefully lit and modernised to provide the town council offices below the courtroom.

There are three hostelries around three sides of the market place. The Burghley Arms (Bull) and Angel had central coaching arches with stables behind. The position of the former ostler's bell can be seen on the right just through the Angel arch and the stables are now a covered precinct of small shops. On the front of the arch is painted , but fading fast, "Inland Revenue Office", below the bay window of the room where dues could be paid on a Saturday morning .

Banks, building societies and estate agents are more common now than central shops. One important shop in Victorian times was Mills' and Baxter in West Street. This was a chemists and druggist with "factory" behind, bottling Mills' table water from a bore. This was an important industry in Victorian times with four other bottling firms Beckett, Lee and Green, Palmer and Smiths. The abundant supply of fresh water in the underground limestone aquifer was also tapped by the Bourne Waterworks Company of 1856 to supply the town from a bore in the front garden of 39a North road. Later the bore in Abbey Road supplied the Spalding Area – some 5 million gallons daily early this century.

BOURNE TABLE WATERS.

(From an Artesian Spring of great depth.)

Soda, Seltzer, Lithia,

Potash,   Lemonade,   Ginger Ale and

Ginger Beer,

As supplied to Royalty, the Nobility and Gentry for over 40 years.

Three Points at Three Periods.

1868 ☞ Dr. Letheby, Government Analyst, pronounced Bourne Water "The Purest in England."

1888 ☞ Dr. Meymott Tidy, Government Analyst—"Bourne Water is of most remarkable purity."

1908 ☞ W. Elborne, Esq., M.A., Cantab., Analyst and Bacteriologist—"Bourne Water from Mills' Factory, an exceedingly bright and clear natural Water of first-class purity— Excellent for drinking purposes."

MILLS' PALE DRY GINGER ALE

Wholesome, refreshing and invigorating. Unequalled for quality, purity and delicacy of flavour. Prepared from Jamaica Ginger Root, with aromatic and tonic ingredients.

MILLS' Bourne Waters can be obtained through all Chemists Wine Merchants, and Hotels, or direct from the Factory in 6 doz. cases carriage paid.

R. M. MILLS & Co.,

The **Original** Artesian Water Factory, **BOURNE.**

56. Bourne Table Waters advertisement.

published in JJ Davies "Historic Bourne" of 1909

57. <u>Mills and Baxter's druggist and chemist West Street.</u>
The Royal coat of arms above the windows denotes the supply of Bourne Waters to Queen Victoria's son the Duke of Connaught and Beccleuch. Arnold's "Boot and shoe warehouse" next door was replaced in 1914 by D Horn outfitter, tailor and hatter.

58. <u>The "Bottling Factory"</u> behind Mills and Baxter. Was it just a row of taps?

59. <u>Mills and Baxter</u> was later taken over by Boots the chemists, who moved next door in the early 1960s, pulling down the elegant building of DH Horn, to replace it with a nondescript shop front and flat roof! Happily Mills and Baxter's building remains, housing a travel agent, a greengrocer and estate agent. The shop on the left is Osbourne's, now Harrison and Dunn's, ironmongers on the corner of South Street.

(Ashby Swift)

60. Surely <u>Mills Bourne Waters</u> were not distributed like this? Perhaps this is a float from the later hospital carnivals simply representing the old firm.

61.The Lee and Green rail tanker used to supply their works in Sleaford. Their artesian bore was in the "old theatre" in the cattle market. On 1st May 1990, when the site was being cleared to take the market stalls off the A15, the bore was exposed and had to be resealed.

62. Lee and Green's offices in the cattle market became Friend's agricultural engineers in 1934, then Davies' builders merchants and was finally cleared in 1989. The man by the door (2nd R) is H Smith, taken on as factory manager when his firm Smith and Co was bought out by Lee and Green in 1917. His son is on the right . The other three (L to R) are Fred Leversidge, Johny James and Nipper Hinson.

(Judges)

63. Cattle Market looking west to the long roof and gable end of the "old theatre", which housed Lee and Green's bottling plant. To the right is the yard of the Bull, now Burghley Arms and to the left the gable end of the Corn Exchange.

(William Pearce, published 1909)

64. Cattle Market pens looking towards Hereward Street. This is now Budgen's car park.

65. <u>Sheep on the move</u> through Morton High Street to new pastures or to the market in Bourne. This must have been a common sight in the town before the prevalence of motor transport.

66. Sheep on display for the auctioneer in <u>Bourne market</u> with a railway porter in the background. No one was without hats in Victorian times, but then they do look as if it was cold.

67. A later <u>sheep sale</u> with the white coated auctioneer Mr Lyall behind and similarly clad, Geo. Gelsthorpe the butcher assessing cuts. A. Holliday's seed merchant's office is behind.

68. <u>Rickard and Sons' agricultural implements</u> in the cattle market has gone but now there is a bedding firm in the shed to the right. The Wesleyan Methodist church on Abbey Road is behind. The advertisement for Mays prize winning manures is partly obscured by Hugh High.

(1934/5)

69. <u>William Friend's agricultural engineers</u> were just across Meadowgate opposite the cattle market, but are now gone.

70. An earlier model of <u>International Harvester tractor</u> possibly as supplied by Foley's, predecessors of Rickards. Binders were the standard machine for harvesting before the coming of combines, which did away with stacking and later threshing.

71. <u>Sneath and Sons of Thurlby</u> with their steam traction engine powering the thresh-ing mill in a neat stackyard. The sound of the traction engine hauling the threshing mill and often a caravan as well, would be common in the roads around Bourne.

(Dennis Morris, Cirencester).

72. <u>Aerial view of 1953</u> showing the Market Place (bottom L) and cattle market pens behind the Methodist Church (bottom R). Friend's engineering sheds are centre picture, beyond is the council housing of George Street and Harrington Street (top), with cress beds between them. The area south of George Street is now the council built Meadow Close com-plex and bungalows.

73. <u>Aerofilm view of Bourne Market Place looking Northwest</u>. The cattle market is behind the Methodist Church in Abbey Road. (bottom right). Notice the rows of out buildings behind the properties in North and West Streets. It is the long terraces of Woodview which stand out, seemingly pointing towards Moody's glasshouses. The fields behind are now built up with housing.

74. <u>A coronation street party outside 24 and 23 Woodview</u> 6th June 1953, featuring in the backrow (left to right) the ladies Barker, Leverton, Atkinson and Ida Pick, Fred Shipley, then Ward, Lunn and Tollower. In front, are Mrs and Mr Bryan and Mrs Bannister.

75. <u>The bore sunk in 1924</u> to supply water to Moody's Glasshouses, showing the considerable artesian pressure of those days. The personalities (L to R) are Tom Rowlett, Percy Wade and Mr and Mrs E.N. Moody, who also had the cress beds by St. Peter's Pool (picture 7)

76. Closer view of <u>Moody's Woodland nurseries</u>, an area which has seen much change. Bottom left the long shed roof of North's yard, one time forage merchants to the Prince of Wales and the Queen. This burned down in September 1986 and the area has been developed as the new Hereward Medical Practice, successor to the Brook Lodge Practice. Across Burghley Street are the grass tennis courts, which became North's garden centre, now closed. The glass houses behind (centre picture) became the houses of Exeter Close. The few houses opposite, across Exeter Street, are demolished now, as are the glasshouses that became Moody's nursery supply yard (bottom left), This area has become a new Sainsbury's store.

49

77. Sheep pens in the Market Place. Looking from West Street at the Town Hall and Rodgers grocers. JJ Clark's with its snow holding fence on the roof edge, which disappeared recently, is now Harrison and Dunn's hardware store on the corner of South Street.

78. Market stalls outside the Bull and Town Hall. It looks like a knife grinder at work in front of the stall. Everyone wearing hats, hence the specialist hatters, such as Todd's, next to the shop with an awning, next to the Angel in picture 79

(published June 1908)

79. <u>The Ostler Memorial in the Market Place</u>. This drinking fountain was built by public subscription in 1860, the year after the death of John Ostler of Cawthorpe. It was designed by Edward Browning, son of Bryan Browning who designed the Town Hall. Ostler must have been highly regarded, no doubt because of his giving land and money to build a primary school in Bourne and land for Dyke school. Pure drinking water would be very reassuring to visitors after the previous year's cholera epidemic among the navvies working on the railways.   (published J T Morris)

80. <u>The Ostler Memorial when on its original stepped plinth</u> later removed to ease traffic. In 1962 the fountain was moved to the cemetery in South Road, where it is today. One can see from the state of the road that this was still the era of horse traffic! Behind the fountain is Osborn's shop now Harrison and Dunn. In West Street the three storied Measures Brothers' grocers is now Coral bookmakers and until recently Bourne Bookworld.

(Redshaw)

81. <u>North Street and The Bull</u> when still intact. The shuttered shop was Todds the hatters, before they moved across to the opposite side of the Market Place (picture 79). In 1880 a bank built over the passage which had led round to the stables at the back of The Bull and took over the end of the Bull itself (next page). It certainly smartened up an untidy corner.

82. <u>William Cecil</u>, born on the site of The Bull in 1520, became Queen Elizabeth's chief minister and first Lord Burghley. As Lord of the Manor of Bourne castle he held the right to hold weekly markets. In his honour the name of the Bull was changed to the Burghley Arms about 1960.

83. <u>The Bank, The Bull and the Town Hall</u> decorated for Queen Victoria's 60th Jubilee in1897. The bank's use of the far end of the Bull is clearly seen. Note the Town Hall clock (see next page)

84. <u>A gang of flax pullers</u> outside the Town Hall in 1920. The hitching posts and railings are still to be seen in front of the steps to the courthouse.
The gangmaster, (the left of three men)was C Pick, with A Pick next. The boy in front of the rear wheel was Tom Waltham with E Maples, arms folded, who became a barber in the shop in Abbey Road, which is now the Prince of Kashmir Indian restaurant.

85. <u>The new Fire Brigade</u> outside the Town Hall in 1900, when the steam pump was kept under the left hand arch and the right one was still the butter market. The horses were stabled in the Bull yard next door. The volunteer firemen were summoned by the fire bell on the Bull chimney, rung by pulling on the rope which can just be seen on the extreme left hanging down behind the railings, out of the reach of children!

86. <u>The fire in the wooden clock tower of the Town Hall</u> on 31st Oct 1933. A Saturday afternoon, when the market stalls had yet to be cleared away. The firebell is to be seen on the Bull chimney and the pulley wheel taking the rope over the parapet. A gas lamp inside the cupola was implicated as the cause of the fire. The clock is now on the pediment below

87. Only in 1932 was the steam fire engine replaced by this <u>model A Ford appliance,</u> seen here outside The Bull. It would be this which dealt with the clock tower fire. The fire brigade captain on the running board is Ivor Reid. On the pavement with the little girl is Mr King, bank manager.

88. <u>The Bull coaching arch</u> through to the stable yard, is now closed off. This looks like the gathering at the Town Hall for the proclamation of 1910. See picture 175.

89. <u>The Lincolnshire regiment parading</u> in front of the Town Hall on 20th May 1915. Spectators taking full advantage of HW Hoyless 1penny and 6 ½ penny bazaar!

90. <u>The Savings Committee</u> for thanksgiving Week 22-29th September 1945, outside the Town Hall. William Friend chairman, with Mr Hudson to his right and Mr and Mrs E D Cooke to his left on the front row.
The target was £50,000 and £ 93,000/16/0 was raised, typical of the town rallying for a good cause.

Chapter 3: South Street, Red Hall and Railway

The oldest surviving domestic building in Bourne is the brick Red Hall off South Street. Probably built as early as 1695 for local landowner Richard Fisher, it belonged to his family until 1730, when it came into the Digby family.

In 1620 William Fisher endowed almshouses for six poor women with a room for a school-master in Watergang Street, now the site of the public toilets in South Street. This may have prompted Thomas Trollope, Lord of the Manor of Bourne Abbots, in his will of 1636 to leave £36 per year to endow six almshouses for poor men, now the Tudor Cottages on South Street bends. He left also £30 per year to pay for his grammar school in the churchyard. Similarly the last Digby at the Red Hall, the widowed Catherine Digby, among other bequests, left money for an annuity for a schoolmistress. After her death in 1836, the Red Hall passed to a relative Sir Philip Pauncefoot Duncombe and it was he who sold the Red Hall and adjacent land to the Bourne and Essendine Railway Company in 1859, when it became part of the station buildings.

The line was taken over by the Great Northern Railway in1864 and in 1866 the Midland and Eastern Railway opened their line to Spalding and the East coast. In 1872 came the Great Northen line to Sleaford and in 1894 the Midland and Great Northen line to Saxby and the West Midlands. In its heyday Bourne was a very busy junction with more than fifty trains per day, over half goods. Such good communications added greatly to Bourne's importance as a centre for agricultural trade. Sadly decline came and by 1930 passenger traffic ceased on the Sleaford line, athough this lasted longest, goods traffic only ceasing in 1964. The Essedine line closed in 1951 and the last passenger traffic ceased in 1959 with the closure of the line to Saxby.

Incredibly the Tudor Red Hall survived, despite so many trains rattling close by for over 100 years and latterly being sorely neglected until acquired by the B.U.C. in 1962. This was largely due to the foresight and tenacity of Councillor Jack Burchnell. After restoration it was opened in 1972 as a community centre for receptions, concerts and meetings, as well as serving as the B.U.C. Office. The station yard was purchased by the old family firm of Wherry and in 1967 the former station warehouse became their pea processing plant. A block of flats was built on their former site in Church Walk and one animal feed warehouse remains in South Street, currently being renovated for Wands.

91. <u>The south side of the Market Place</u> with Gant's the saddlers, now Dinky Shop, next to the Nag's Head. The wooden horse in the window went off to the Klondyke horse sanctuary, near the brickpits south of West Road. The cottage with three dormer windows beyond the awning in South Street is the site of William Fisher's alms houses for six poor women, now the public toilets.

92. <u>The Market Place leading to Abbey road</u>. A faded but early picture as it shows the Ostler drinking fountain on its original steps, as erected in 1860 but before the 1870 building of the Corn Exchange. Yet another three dormer cottage and the first Post Office were demolished for its entrance. Note how the Nag's head building overshadows the thatched shop that preceeded the three storey block on the corner of South Street.

93 . <u>Sheep pens around the Ostler Fountain</u> in the Market Place before the demolition of Shippeys shop to build the three storey block on the corner. There is a fine assortment of characters, some of whom must be on the steps of the drinking fountain. The Nag's Head has been rebuilt since the previous picture.

94. Mr and Mrs A. C. Barnatt outside their <u>hairdressing shop</u> just around the corner in South Street at the end of the three storey corner block. This is now Neal's hairdressers.

95. <u>Palmer's saddlery shop</u> on the west side of South Street, an important service in the days of horse transport. The building is unchanged but recently served a need of our times, as Lincolnshire Bow double glazing and PVC doors and windows.

96. <u>A parade in South Street</u> to celebrate Queen Victoria's diamond jubilee of 1897. The three storey building on the right was a Temperance Hotel, now a Chinese restaurant next to the Mason's Arms.

97. <u>Ashby Swift's Riverside Studio</u> in South Street with the Mason's Arms behind and the Angel hotel in the distance. The Red Lion is across the street, and Johnson Brothers (late PJ Clark) shoeing forge and implement works behind. This became the site of the Darby and Joan Hall of 1959

98. The presentation of the <u>first WVS van</u> in 1963 outside the Darby and Joan Hall. Now the W.R.V.S., the local organiser then was Mrs V. Wherry, seen here with Mrs M Wilson, from the Lincoln office and Mrs Tippler, UDC chairman. The fundraisers behind the van are (L to R) Ted Wilson (Wherrys social club), J Mason (clerk to UDC), Rev JC Husk (United Reform Church), Reg Sones (Tuck Bros), J H Moody (fire officer), and Ernie Robinson (ambulance officer).

99. <u>Wherrys Cottage on the East side of South Street</u> when W P Birds wagon from Pasture Hill farm overturned. The bearded man on the cart shaft is Sam Futer wagon maker of Auster Lodge.

The railings along the riverside nearly disappeared in the 1960s but happily were saved so one can still enjoy the ducks on the Eau and the colourful flower beds of the Memorial gardens when stuck in a car waiting for the traffic lights!

100 <u>Wherrys Cart</u> drawn by "Flower" outside the feedstuff bagging warehouse on the corner of Church Walk. This was pulled down, although the less attractive warehouse next to it survives.

101. <u>Inside Wherry's feedstuff warehouse</u>, which transferred to the station site in 1967.

102 <u>Bag stitching in Wherrys warehouse</u>, South Street.

103. <u>A Sunday School Parade in South Street</u> near Baldock's Mill, showing the two warehouses of Wherry's and a thatched summer house in The Cedars' garden.

104 <u>A 1953 aerial view of South Street</u> with the Market Place at the top and the Wherry's warehouse which was demolished at the bottom. Abbey Road curves off to the right with the entrance tower and long roof of the Corn Exchange behind.
On the extreme left is the Eau before it was bridged for the car park and extreme right is the site of the Abbey House kitchen gardens, where the Church Hall was to be built. Central top is the Nags Head yard, with Wherrys' yard below, on the north side of Church Walk. The pea processing shed on the right was demolished for a block of flats.

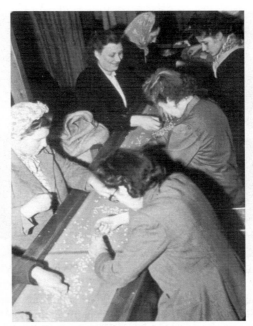

105 <u>Pea picking in Wherry's,</u> Church Walk, just after the second World War. The firm began dried pea marketing in 1878. Initially packed in workers' homes, this was concentrated in the Church Walk factory built in 1902, then transferred to the old Station yard in 1967, where it is wholly automated.

106 <u>Modern pea sorting machines</u> in 1982 in the old railway storage and transit warehouse. Adrian Morgan crouching and James Wherry standing. Peas go to wholesale grocers, supermarkets, canners and caterers all over the world, especially to the Far East.

107 <u>Wherrys directors </u>in March 1966 (L to R) DJ Randall, VFC Wherry, EK Wherry, AW Wherry and PY Wherry. The firms founder Edward Wherry is pictured on the wall. Proprietor of the village store in Edenham, in 1806 he bought the premises of John Gibson on both sides of North Street, the transaction carried out by William Worth soliciter (photo 226) - for a retail then wholesale grocery business. His grandson WR Wherry added the seed grain business and pea processing (photo 104)

108 <u>Wherry's pea factory</u> in the old railway warehouse on the station site, south of the Red Hall, seen from Whatton's wood yard in what was the SE corner of the pleasure gardens of the Red Hall.

(McG May 1975)

109 <u>Navvies laying rails</u>. So named as the itinerant work force which moved around the country digging out the canals(navigations) in the 18th century, moved to the railways in the 19th century and roads in the 20th century. Local labourers must have been recruited also, as the man with foot on spade, first right middle row, is W.J. Allit of Bourne.

110 <u>The Red Hall</u> of about 1600 which became railway offices for the Bourne Essendine Railway of 1860. The ground floor room to the left of the porch was the ticket office, now the Trustees' office of Bourne United Charities and that to the right of the porch was the waiting room, now the WEA classroom. The station warehouse and huge yew tree remain but the outbuildings and water tower have gone.

(picture before 1894)

111 <u>An early steam train in front of the Red Hall.</u> Much heavier engines and up to 50 trains a day were to rattle past the Red Hall for over 100 years.

112 <u>Bourne station staff</u> on the island platform, with the footbridge of 1894 which crossed the line between the Red Hall and island platform.

113 <u>The Red Hall platform</u> before the 1894 footbridge over the line to the island platforms whose canopy is seen right. The sundial is still in the south face of the Red Hall, but the out buildings, platforms and railway lines have gone.

114 <u>The island platforms</u> looking west. The engine sheds are to be seen on the right. The billboards advertise return tickets to Skegness for 7s 3d and Hunstanton for 7s 6d, with links to Holt, Sherringham, Cromer and Yarmouth. This was shortly before passenger traffic ceased in 1959.

(Judge)

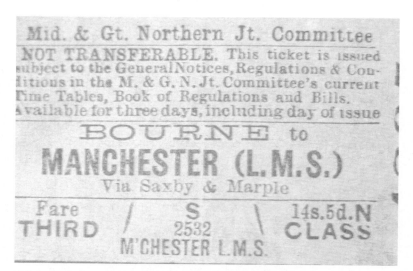

Mid. & Gt. Northern Jt. Committee

NOT TRANSFERABLE. This ticket is issued subject to the General Notices, Regulations & Conditions in the M. & G. N. Jt. Committee's current Time Tables, Book of Regulations and Bills. Available for three days, including day of issue

BOURNE to

MANCHESTER (L.M.S.)

Via Saxby & Marple

Fare / S \ 14s.5d.N
THIRD / 2532 \ CLASS

M'CHESTER L.M.S.

115 <u>A ticket</u> from Bourne to Manchester, the route lost in 1959.

116 <u>The engine sheds and turntable</u> with the water tower on the edge of the picture, taken when demolition had begun. The turntable is now at Wansford station on the Nene Valley line but had to be lengthened to take some of the continental engines transferred there. The water tower was so well built it took five attempts to blow it up.

117 <u>The last passenger train,</u> the 9.20pm from Spalding on 28th February 1959, attracted some 94 customers when it had been carrying an average of four in the months before. This picture is looking west from the footbridge with the station warehouse on the left. Chalked on one of the carriages is "Death to the M&GN", sometimes known as the "muddle and go nowhere"! The two Bourne brothers in the foreground are John (dark coat) and Arthur Ulyatt (light mac), electrician and cabinet maker respectively.

118 <u>Demolition of the island platform</u> in March 1964, showing how close the line was to the Red Hall.

119 <u>Bourne Station</u> from the south west in 1959, showing the many lines of this important junction. In the background (L to R) is Baldock's Mill, Brook Lodge in front of the Abbey Church and the Red Hall.

(Summerfield)

120 <u>The East Signal Box and South Street level crossing</u> with the twin gables of the crossing keeper's cottage, seen behind the cattle loading platform. Beyond the crossing is the embankment across the Abbey Lawn carrying the line to Sleaford. In the foreground is a station lamp on the east end of the island platform. Happily four of the station lamps have been preserved by Andrew Cooke and can be seen down the drive of The Croft on North Road.

121 <u>A steam train leaving the station,</u> on the line to Sleaford, seen from the South Street level crossing. Probably a Patrick Sterling 240 pictured before 1900.

122 <u>The east signal box and South Street crossing</u> seen from Brook Lodge. Beyond the crossing gate is the crossing keeper's cottage last occupied by Mr. Knight before its demoloition. Right is Gray's farm cottage. The end of the Tudor Cottages with the three storey Cavalry House is on the left.

(Holloway)

123 <u>The division of the lines</u> seen from the Church tower looking East. Across the picture is the 1872 Sleaford line of the GNR, crossing Notleys mill pond on a wooden bridge and skirting the Abbey lawn on an embankment. On the right is the 1866 M and ER line curving towards the Austerby level crossing then on to Spalding. The monk's garden in the foreground was to become the grass courts of the tennis club, with the open air swimming pool beyond (see picture 29).

(published 1909)

124 <u>The Austerby level crossing and footbridge</u> with Edward Garfoot on the Spalding line.

(Garfoot)

125 <u>The Austerby</u> looking west towards the level crossing, with the footbridge out of sight behind the terrace of houses on the right. The view is barely changed today but for the gates, pedestrians and state of the road!

(Ashby Swift)

126 <u>The post war Swimming Pool</u> looking East toward the embanked Sleaford line. The Spalding Road gasholder can be seen in the left background. The diving boards had to go when it was realised that the depth of the pool was inadequate for safety. Much of the lawn has gone with increased paving around the pool and there are far fewer flower beds but a real effort is still made to keep the pool attractive,with Dick Sellar's lovely hanging baskets under the canopy this side of the Monk's wall.

127 <u>The Abbey Road railway bridge</u> with Spalding Road gas holder beyond. The trees obscure the school. The youngsters are Rachael Cliffe with her doll, Robert and Caroline High behind with Timothy Royce on the right.

(High)

128 <u>Demolition of the Abbey Road rail bridge</u> in 1965, looking from the Spalding Road side with the Abbey Road Primary School beyond.

129 <u>The Abbey Road Primary School</u> with the Sleaford line embankment behind. Originally this was the Star Lane elementary school built in 1877 by the School Board. It is little changed but for the loss of the bell tower and Headmaster's house. One famous head was JJ Davies author of "Historic Bourne" published in 1909. In 1991 it was the first primary school to become Grant Maintained, under head Bob Wright.

(William Pearce)

130 <u>The infant class</u> at the primary school about 1900. Too attractive a group to leave out despite the broken glass stuck to the front of the photograph.

131 Labelled "<u>Bourne Grammar School 1880</u>?", this must be the whole school outside the building in the churchyard. Incredibly the names are given (left to right) backrow T Branston, G Mays, A Webber, William Webber (head), T Webber, C Burn, W Cresswell, C Longstaff and front row A S Allen, J Longstaff, A Chamberlain, A Mays, A Webber, F Glover, A Mays, A Brown, and A Smith. Many familiar names in Bourne's history.

132 <u>The old Grammar School in the Churchyard</u>. Most probably the site of the school founded by the 2nd Lord of the Manor of Bourne Abbots, ThomasTrollope in 1636. Endowed with £30 per year to pay " an honest learned and Godly master", usually the post was filled by the Vicar of the time.

133 <u>South Street bend</u> showing (L to R) Gray's farm cottage, Brook Lodge, the Abbey Church, Tudor cottages and Cavalry House. The last named in honour of Thomas Rawnsley, wool merchant, who lived here during the Napoleonic Wars. He raised a troop of horse as mounted home guard in case of invasion, which never came.

(Valentine 46806)

134 <u>Road mending on South Street</u> in front of Cavalry House. Behind the water cart are the four dormer windows of the Tudor Cottages, endowed in 1636 with £36 per year by Thomas Trollope as almshouses for six poor men, but now two homes.

135 <u>An aerial view of the Abbey Church area</u>. Gray's farm cottage and Baldock's mill left, the South Street bends with the Memorial Garden and Wellhead Park beyond. The old Grammar School in the Churchyard and grass tennis courts in the Monks' garden. Wherry's yards behind the Church with the South Street car park and Warner's printing works beyond. On the right the vicarage, with the Eau cutting across the garden. Beyond that, is Abbey Road curving north to the market place.

136 <u>Gray's farm cottage</u> opposite Brook Lodge on the South Street bends in July 1975. It was remarkable that a small working farm yard should remain so close to the centre of town. The 250 year old mud and stud cottage was demolished in January 1977.

137 I just missed photographing Mrs Gray talking to the firemen from her upstairs window when South Street was flooded after heavy rain, a penalty for building on the original course of a stream. Flash floods were common until recent years. Tuck's garage can be seen beyond the fire tender.

(McG 21 Mar 1968)

138 Tuck's garage staff with a Clynomaster motor cycle. Saville Turner is on the extreme left. This was the site of the Footpath Gate into the Red Hall grounds, demolished in 1918 by prisoners of war.

Chapter 4:East of town, chiefly Spalding and Abbey Roads

Much in this area has already been covered by pictures of the river and railways but there are still some family businesses for example Delaine's buses and Stroud's laundry, yet to be featured. Otherwise it is simply a trip form The Austerby to Bedehouse Bank and the Spalding Road, returning by Manning Road and Abbey Road to the market place, the scene of many parades over the years.

139 The studio in the garden of <u>Shillaker House</u> which was demolished to build the council flats of Shillaker Court in the Austerby.

140 A 1929 picture of <u>Mrs Shillaker in her studio</u>. The girl in the full length portrait hanging behind the vase of pampas grass was the daughter of Mr. J.W. Lake, cabinet maker. I saw the picture in his widow's house in West Road, before it was demolished to build Manor Court.

141 <u>The Austerby street party</u> on V.E. Day, 8 May 1945

142 <u>The Eastgate Mission Church</u> in Willoughby Road, demolished for bungalows next to Booth's garage.

143 <u>Inside the Anglican Eastgate Mission Church.</u> The lecturn came from the Abbey Church when replaced in 1902.

144 <u>Miss Adam's cottage in Bedehouse Bank</u> for which Rod Hoyle, art master at the Grammar School, formed the Bourne Civic Society in 1978, in an unsuccessful attempt to save a once common mud and stud cottage.

(posted 23/5/1980)

145 <u>The Butcher's Arms Inn in Eastgate</u> with Mrs Lappage and daughter outside. In May 1941 a Junkers Ju 88 was shot down by a Beaufighter from R.A.F. Wittering. The crash demolished the building, killing the Licensee, S. Boulton his wife and two relatives, as well as three soldiers of the Lancashire Loyals billeted there. Of the crew of four, only the Gunner survived baling out. Jack Lovell's garage was built on the site and when excavating to instal a fuel tank in September 1964 an unexploded 1,100lb bomb was unearthed among some wreckage of the plane. It was unexploded as the plane was heading for Belfast.

146 <u>The great flood of 1910</u> when the Glen bank burst at Tongue End inundating Bourne fen. Here looking along the Spalding Road towards Twenty. This was not unusual before the days of the Internal Drainage Board. This three mile stretch of straight road was very useful to RM when testing racing cars pre-war!

147 <u>Bog oaks</u> turned up by deep ploughing on Bourne North fen, as the dark peat is used up and the soil level falls. Not all are oaks but are remains of trees from the forest that was here before inundation from the sea in prehistoric times. This view is south from Spalding Road towards the embanked Eau.

(mcg July 1992)

148 <u>The pinfold</u> to hold stray cattle and sheep was on Spalding Road. Seen here (looking SW) as one approached the Maltings behind Eastgate House and the gasworks chimney which can be seen through the trees.

149 Aerial view of <u>the environs of Eastgate House</u> in the 1970s. Looking over May's garage forecourt and the Splading Road to (L to R) the Delaine Bus Company sheds, the old malting and engine test house of ERA days then the long gas works building of BRM fame. Centre is Eastgate House with RM's yellow Rover in the yard by the back door and his walled garden on the West side of the outbuildings.

Left of centre is the yard of Gelsthorpe's butcher's shop. The chesnut trees behind are alongside the Eau running down Eastgate with the white Brook House on the site of the council flats of Worth Court. Behind is Booth's garage and the three blocks of Owen Court, against the curve of Willoughby Road.

150 The Delaine Bus Company is a family business descended from William Smith who began a horse and cart passenger service in 1890. In 1902 they acquired premises in Spalding Road, adding motor taxis in 1910 and their first bus in 1919. This bus in the livery of <u>TA Smith crashed into Kate's Bridge</u> on 2nd August 1930, on route to Peterborough. Happily no one was injured and the bus was rebuilt and in use until 1952.

151 In 1939 the bus depot was enlarged by taking over some of the ERA works alongside, but during the war these premises were requisitioned to billet paratroops, then land army girls. The company became <u>Delaine Coaches Limited</u> in 1941. In 1959 with the decline in the railways, private hire grew. This Delaine Bus, JP 6979, built in 1948 and retired in 1960, is seen with an outing from Morton.

152 <u>Demolition of some of the gasworks buildings</u> 22nd January 1960. Looking NW from the Eastgate side towards the gasholder across the Spalding Road.

153 Setting up the <u>BRM workshops</u> on the gas works site in April 1960. This is where the last of the BRMs were displayed 21 years later, before going for sale at Christie's (see picture 47). Now it is an auctioneers' hall itself.

154 Looking towards the Church from the Recreation ground. The terraces of council houses on Manning Road on the left and the chimney possibly in Whatton's Yard on the extreme right.

(posted Sept 1916)

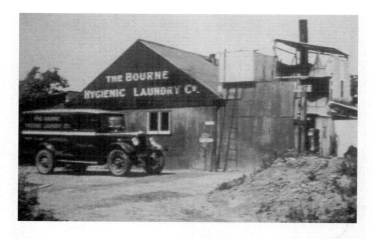

155 Another family firm, the Bourne Hygenic Laundry Company in Manning Road, was begun in 1932 by Mr. Stroud in what had been the site of Whatton's woodyard.

(about 1934)

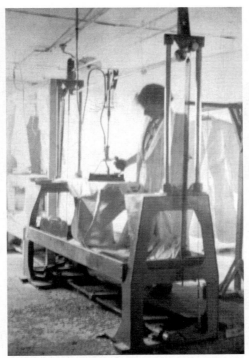

156 Basil Stroud's pre-war prize winning gas press.

157 Inside Bourne Laundry the Mayor and Mayoress, Councillor and Mrs J Wright being shown some of their newest equipment by Basil and Stuart Stroud. The firm employed over 600 staff in the 1960s with shops in eight towns in the district. (1969/70)

158 <u>Abbey Road looking West,</u> with Nowell's whitewashed cottage and R Cheers' tiny shop, which were demolished to make way for Nowell's Lane.

159 JR Walker's shoeing and general <u>smithy in Abbey Road</u>

160 <u>Oddfellows parade in Abbey Road.</u> The town band is opposite the Light Dragoon with a second banner outside the Marquis of Granby, in the distance.

161 <u>Abbey Road shops</u> Hemsell's baker and confectioner and Hodgson's furnishing and ironmongery shop, this side of the Light Dragoon Inn. Possibly 1912, the same parade as picture 164.

(Redshaw)

162 The same scene in <u>Abbey Road</u> as the Oddfellows parade, but during a flash flood on 3 September 1931.

163 Lorenzo Warner at the door of his <u>newsagents shop in Abbey Road</u>. In 1920 he bought Morris' shop and print works in West Street. Later still he bought the maltings further along West street. Note the billboard - Mussolini was shot but not seriously hurt by Violet Gibson, Daughter of an Irish Peer on 7th April 1926.

164 <u>The Congregational Sunday School of 1912</u> in Abbey Road. This was the heyday of church attendance, when the Congregational Sunday School had over 150 on roll. The highlight of the year was the annual parade from Willoughby Road to the Wellhead or Park Field in the Austerby for games and a picnic.

165 <u>The Congregational Sunday School</u> parading past the Light Dragoon in Abbey Road with the Town Band behind their banner.

(posted July 1912)

166 <u>The Congregational Sunday School parade pausing in the Market Place</u> possibly in 1912 also. The trade of the hatters must have been flourishing at this time.

167 <u>The Wesleyan Methodist Sunday School Treat on the Wellhead Field</u> west of St Peter's Pool in 1914.

168 <u>The Congregational Treat of 1914 in the Park Field</u> now with adult fancy dress and decorated floats. The man holding the reins looks like JJ Davies the Abbey Road Primary School headmaster.

169 Another picture from the Congregational Treat of 1914 this time of a decorated lorry load. Is it JJ Davies again?

170 A still more elaborate Congregational fete on the Park Field Austerby. The crown suggests this may have been about 22 June 1911, the coronation of George V.

171 Soldiers preceeding the <u>Oddfellows banner in Abbey Road</u> having just left the Market Place, possibly in the parade of 1910 for the proclamation of King George V. This was a great age for parades and many reasons were found to have them.

172 The same view of <u>Abbey Road towards the Market Place</u> in earlier times. Coale's bazaar and fancy goods warehouse of this picture, has been modernised and became Hodson's ironmonger and gun smith in the picture above. The awning beyond is that of the London Co-operative Meat Company.

173 <u>Coale's the butchers of Abbey Road</u> was virtually in the Market Place. George and Harriet Coale are in front of the shop, with their adopted son George Gann on the left cart and Harry Bentham with the knife. The Corn Exchange can be seen behind the second cart. EEC hygiene regulations were some years away!

174 An early <u>pedestrian crossing and miniroundabout in the Market Place</u>. Coale's butchers shop is the white building between Roger's grocers and the Corn Exchange across Abbey Road from the Nag's Head. (Compare picture 92).

(William Pearce published in 1909)

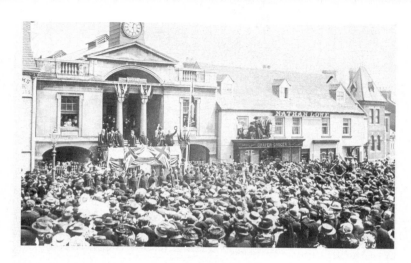

175 <u>The Market Place thronged for the Proclamation of King George V in 1910</u> with every vantage point in use.

176 Another view of the <u>Market Place on Proclamation day 1910</u>, looking towards Abbey road, with the Oddfellows banner. Scouts began in 1908 but Bourne already had some on parade. The tall man with a moustache in the centre (behind the last Scout on the right) is JJ Davies, headmaster of the Abbey Road primary school and author of "Historic Bourne "published in 1909.

177 Only a solitary scout is to be seen in front of this parade through the market place for the <u>Peace celebrations after the first World War</u>. The town band and Oddfellows banner brings up the rear, behind what looks like the demobilised soldiers.

178 The <u>Girl Guides photographed outside the vicarage</u> in 1921. This is till a flourishing movement with 2 Rainbow, 3 Brownie, 2 Guide and 1 Senior Section unit meeting regularly in the Shippon Barn (picture 11)

The girl 6th from the right in the front row, is Sheila MacLeod of Cawthorpe who married Trevor Brodrick. Both were totally deaf lip readers. Their home Frogmore Cottage on North Road had a paddock and hut they allowed the Guides to use as headquarters and camp site. Trevor inherited the titles Lord Midleton and Baron Brodrick of Frogmore and it was as Lady Midleton that Sheila ended her days as a resident of this old vicarage, now The Cedars residential home.

Chapter 5: West Street and Road leading to the brickpits and Klondyke

Once a populous part of town down Manor Lane, skirting round the west of the castle site, there was a disasterous fire in this area on 23rd August 1605, which lasted three days and left no house standing. King James I proclaimed it a disaster and authorised aid from collections far afield. It is to the S.W. beyond Manor Lane that a further 2,000 houses are planned!

179 The Market Place in the days when either a photographer or traffic must have been unusual! Winter must have been harder too, as suggested by the snow fence on the roof parapet of Johnson's on the left.

(Redshaw)

180 Johnson Bros hardware and ironmongers on the corner of South and West Streets, with an interesting selection of wares out on the pavement.

181 The 2<u>nd</u> Battalion of the Lincolnshire Regiment marching down West street from the Wellhead "trenches" on the 2nd April 1891.
On the left Arnold's shop next to the Ropewalk arch. On the right Measures' grocery with a brewer's dray and the milkfloat in front, Home milk deliveries were usual but not in bottles, rather ladled from the churn into the householder's jug.

182 The north side of <u>West Street decorated for Queen Victoria's diamond (60<u>th</u>) jubilee</u> of 1897. From right, Osborn's bakery, another three dormered cottage which has gone; Major Bell's solicitors, which is now the TSB without the first floor bay windows; the Crown Inn, now a shop with shopping precinct behind; the Horse and Groom, now Costcutters grocery store; then the 17th C Monkstone House formerly Jack Raynor's home, now the Balti King Indian Restaurant.

183 <u>The Town Hall from West Street</u>. On the left the Crown Inn and Major Bell's solicitors. On the right Pick's Chocolate Box bakery beside the rope walk just beyond Warners newsagents with the printworks behind, now Martin McColl newsagents shop and Kinnsway furnshings behind.

(posted 1932)

184 <u>Heidelberg printing Machine</u> with Barry Hunt in the works behind Warner's shop, now moved to the old Maltings and St. Peter's hospital further along West Street.
Warners Midlands plc is now a multi million magazine printing firm with the latest computerised equipment still run by Lorenzo's son Michael and his two sons Stephen and Philip. Michael has just been honoured with the MBE in this year's Honours List.

185 <u>A Hospital Carnival float</u> of Hereward the Wake just outside the Crown, with Major Bell's solicitors' office and Osborn's bakery behind. Photographed by Ashby Swift from his West Street studio, to which he moved from the Riverside Studio in South Street.

186 Mr McIntyre in a garden near the Baptist Church as <u>John Bull for a hospital fete</u>. These were an annual event very necessary to raise funds for The Butterfield Cottage hosptial which was wholly financed voluntarily. Not quite the build of the traditional John Bull, he was right for his job as usher at the Magistrate's Court.

(Ashby Swift)

187 "Our Brave Volunteers" with Recruiting Sargeant Todd in 1914 in front of the Chapel House, West street, next to the Baptist Church, set back out of sight on the right. From left to right, the names are listed as Bloodworth (gasworks manager), unknown, Meakins, unkown, Gilbert (boy), unkown, Sherwin, Baldock, Bloodworth, unknown, Darnes, Vickers, and Savage.

188 West Street towards the Maltings. On the left Saxonhurst, recently refurbished as the Registrar's Office, Tabor's shop and the Golden Lion. On the right, Cliffe's little shop with the protruding sign, was formerly the recruiting office of the 2nd Battalion of the Lincs Volunteer Regiment. Part of the sign is still to be seen above the window. The Chapel House and cottage were being demolished for the 1981 Post Office. Beyond them the bay windowed house survives. This was Stubley's, the scenery painter for theatrical shows in the district.

189 <u>The Bourne Amateurs'</u> production of Gilbert and Sullivan's "Pirates of Penzance" in January 1914. Cast members listed as, (L to R) Sgt. Of Police, Mr Wallis; Edith and Isabel, Misses Fowler and Swift; Samuel, Mr Hartley; Mabel, Miss Hartshorn (Abbey Road, teacher); Frederick, Mr Pearson. (bottom) Pirate King, Mr Fowler; Ruth, Miss Stubley and Major General Stanley, Mr Nichols (South Street baker). (Ashby Swift)

190 <u>Bourne Operatic Society</u>'s Balkan Princess of November 1932. The scenery was probably painted by Stubley. The town has two excellent amateur dramatic groups today, the Bourne Players and Bourne Footlights, but no operatic society

191 <u>The West Street Institute</u> in a building of 1872, on the corner of St Peter's Road looking south east. Founded in 1896 for "the healthy recreation, education and intellectual improvement of its members" it provided a library, music, debates, biliards and other games. It still flourishes as the Pyramid billiards club. The house next door, Hurn House, was saved from demolition by Clifford Hirst.

(published 1909)

BOURNE VOLUNTEER TRAINING CORPS.

192 <u>Bourne Volunteer Training Corps outside the Rifle Club</u> minature range in the basement behind the Institute in St Peter's Road.

(Ashby Swift, posted 19 May 1916)

193 <u>North's Yard</u> in December 1986 after the fire of September which burned out the barn. This family firm supplied hay and straw to the Royal Mews in London, hence the Royal Warrants for the Queen and Prince of Wales. The yard became the site of the Hereward Group Practice premises which opened in December 1998. This group is successor to Dr Holloway's practice of Brook Lodge. It shared the Health Centre premises in St. Gilbert's Road with the Galletly practice group from North Road, from 1971 to 1998.

194 <u>The tennis courts in Burghley Street</u> behind Norths's yard, looking SW towards the Maltings in West Street. Recently this has been Michael Norths's garden centre but it is now closed. The group of convalescent first World War wounded were nursed by the Red Cross in the National School and Vestry Hall in North Street during the First World War. (picture 234)

195 <u>A Home Guard group in the Burghley Street tennis courts</u> during the second World War. See picture 76.

196 Another second World War group, <u>The Savings Committee outside the Town Hall</u> in 1943. The target was clearly Hitler, rather than £111, 441/17s /5d, which must have been the commendable but odd total raised.
Extreme left is Mr Stanton, Clerk to B.U.C. back row right Mr Hudson, bank manager and seated extreme right Mrs Ida Pick of the Red Cross.

197 <u>West Street looking west</u> with the turning to Exeter Street immediately to the right and beyond houses many of which have gone for the Police Station and Manor Court. On the left Stamford House, next a thatched cottage, a pantiled house, and the gable end of the old Maltings building, before the turn into Manor Lane. The Manor House Hostel on the far corner, was the hostel for nurses of the Butterfield and isolation hospitals but is now flats.

198 The 2nd Lincolnshire Volunteer Regiment <u>cycle detachment marching</u> down West Street and turning into Manor Lane to go to the Wellhead "trenches". Possibly June 1905. On the left most of the cottages have gone for the Police Station. On the right is the front of the old Maltings, housing Warner's (Midlands) plc state of the art print machines.

199 <u>The Alms Houses in West Road</u> run by the trustees of the Bourne United Charities since 1931. The funds come chiefly from the Robert Harrington charity, a gift of farm land on the outskirts of London which developed as Leytonstone Properties. Apart from the twelve almshouses there is a weekly allowance for over two hundred elderly Brunnians from the Essex fund.

200 <u>The West Road Villas</u> the nearest of which bears the date 1885. The grocers cart is Cliffe's from West Street, now Cliffe's furnishing and removal business. Land behind the villas was sold to build the Westfield primary school in 1977.

201 <u>Navvies in the brickpits south of West Road</u>, an important source of local clay for the building of Bourne. The soil of most gardens is heavy, but the fen edge on the east of the town has light peaty soil.

202 <u>The Klondyke horse sanctuary</u> near the brickfields started by the "International League for the Prevention of Export of Live Horses". A considerable food trade to the continent at one time. They provided a home for elderly or disabled horses unfit for work, until such a time as they need to be put down humanely in the abattoir, run from 1932 by the Mays firm from Eastgate! The wooden horse came from Gant's saddlery shop in the Market Place (see picture 91).

Chapter 6: North Street and North Road

This is the main shopping street of the town with the Angel Precinct and Burghley centre off it. Sadly there have been several empty shops in recent years and although we already have Budgen's and a Rainbow superstore, a Sainsbury superstore has just opened in Exeter street on Moody's Nursery Supplies site. (pictures 73 to 76)

The road is the A15 imperceptibly rising to the slight ridge of Mill Drove where Wherry's mill stood until struck by lightning in the first World War. Traffic has increased relentlessly in recent years, but there is no sign of the much needed by-pass. Though I saw a proposed western bypass marked on a town plan in 1961, later building to the northwest has been allowed on this route. At least the market stalls were taken off the A15 to safety behind the Town Hall in 1989

203 The Market Place stalls looking north up the A15. The Delaine bus coming south is baulked by the van delivering at Hiltons shoe shop, not to mention a van parked on double yellow lines outside the old Post Office, recently an off licence. On the extreme left, on the site of Measures' grocers (picture 181), Spires electricians, is now Catours travel agents.

(posted 23 May 1980)

204 The Market Place on market day, a Thursday in the 1960s when there were still Hodgkinson's auctions "on the stones" outside the Town Hall. Virtually anything would be sold from bicycles to budgies, with agricultural tools, game and market garden produce predominating. The auctioneer was usually George Knipe, Cecil Hodgkinson's partner. The Delaine bus from Haconby looks empty and probably heading back to the depot in Spalding Road.

205 North Street in much quieter times when the town pump (water not petrol) was still to be seen (left) and the Bank had not yet been built on Todd's old shop and the Bull passage (extreme right).

206 <u>The old Post Office</u> was between Lloyd's Bank and Hilton's shoe shop and was recently an off licence. It moved to West Street in 1981. The billboard is advertising the annual Bourne and district ploughing match, with prizes of £40 on 11 October 1903.

207 <u>The first hospital rag day parade</u> in July 1929 passing the old Post Office with Hilton's shoe shop and the International Stores and Judges shop beyond. The rider, HG Pinfold preceding the town band was representing Lady Godiva's famous ride through Coventry! Her son Hereward, "the Wake", was reputedly born in Bourne's castle. These annual fund raising events were essential to support the entirely voluntary Butterfield hospital. The 1929 event raised 64 pounds 16 shillings and 3 pence!

208 <u>Roberts shop</u>, later Judges the chemist and Wherry's grocers with the bow window, were demolished to build the Burghley centre. This picture was taken before 1883 when Wherry's office block was built on the garden beyond the grocery shop, where we see the open gate in the fence. One can just see the barber's pole on the shop beyond.

209 <u>North street decorated for Queen Victoria's diamond (60th) Jubilee in 1897</u>. Wherry's office block is now inserted between their grocery shop and the barber's beyond. It too was demolished for the Burghley Centre.

210 <u>Inside Judge's chemist shop</u> in the days of gas lighting. Yardley's old English lavender lady is beside the case of spectacles - "Bruce Green's sight savers". Utensils for home nursing are in the bottom cupboard beside the feeding cups.

211 <u>Mr Tory the candlemaker</u> for Wherry's first grocers and drapers on the west side of North Street acquired in 1806 by the founder of the family firm Edward Wherry (picture 107). It was rebuilt in 1840 as the Central buildings and later sold to Peterborough Co-operative Society.

212 A 1963 <u>aerial view of North Street and the cattle market</u> behind, the area which has been developed as the Burghley Centre with Budgen's store and car park. The shop fronts to be seen are (from right to left) Robert's, later Judge's chemists; Wherry's grocery shop and office with the long yard and retail grocery behind; Stevenson's barbers; Pick's forge; and part of Pearce's china and jewellers.

213 Edward <u>Wherry and Sons' wholesale grocery dispatch warehouse</u> founded by Edward Wherry's sons in the early 1800s, when goods from London and Manchester often came by boat. At the same time coastal steamers carried peas to Glasgow and wheat to Leith from WR Wherry and Co the agricultural side of the family business.

214 <u>Stevenson's barbers</u> between Pick's forge and Wherry's office block. This too was demolished in the 1960s to build Toulson and Spencer's hardware shop, recently B and T wallpaper.

215 <u>Stevenson's barbers next to Stock's garage</u>, formerly Pick's forge. Imagine the hold up on the A15 when the petrol pump arm was swung out over the road. Painted down both sides of the building can still be seen, although fading, the words 'STOCKS LTD'. The sunlight is catching the dormer windows of the cottage in the distance which was demolished for the Tudor Cinema.

216 <u>Pick's forge with Pearce's china and jewellery shop beyond.</u> This became Stock's garage then Davies ironmongers. Recently Miniatures, the doll's house shop, was under the arch.

217 <u>The site of the Burghley Centre entrance</u> pictured about 1965 before the demolition (from R to L) of Judge's chemists, the Antique shop, Wherry's grocery shop and offices. Beyond is Toulson and Spencer's hardware, recently B and T Wallpaper, on the site of Stevenson's barbers, then Davies ironmongers, with Stock's name to be seen on the side of the building.

(JJ Redshaw)

121

218 <u>The west side of North Street</u> looking back towards the Market place with Parmiter's shop (right) next to Smith's family grocers, established in 1857.

(Redshaw)

219 <u>The interior of Smith's grocers shop</u> in December 1998 just before closure after, more than 100 years of the family business.
Judy and John Smith with Pat Hand.

(McG)

220 <u>Smith's shop</u> is behind the gas lamp, with the Six Bell's and Old Windmill pubs beyond. The man reading the billboard is outside Knott's sweetshop, with Smith's fish shop next to Smith's Grocers

(Ashby Swift)

221 Looking back down <u>North Street towards the Market Place</u>. On the left V. Walls and sons' outfitters, Pearce's and Stock's. On the right the Six Bells, an unkown shop , then Smiths Grocers.

222 <u>The Six Bells</u> licensed to let horses and traps and Redshaw's the photographic shop from which several of our pictures have come.

(Redshaw)

223 <u>An early Redshaw plate.</u> The Gladstone bag suggests this is a doctor.

(Redshaw)

224 Another Redshaw photo of <u>a Private School group</u>, possibly one of those in West Street.

(Redshaw)

225 Labelled a <u>prize "sheep of 285"lb</u>, one of the most unusual plates.

(Redshaw)

226 <u>The Old Windmill Inn and the house of Worth's,</u> the solicitor who lived here in 1825, when his son Charles Frederick was born. He soon had to leave because of business problems and did not return till 1860. His son had to make his own way in life from the age of 11 when he started at a local printers. Next year he was apprenticed in millinery at Swan and Edgar in London. Aged 20 and not speaking French he went to Paris eventually joining Gagelin and Opizez suppliers of silk to the court dressmakers of Napoleon 3rd.

(Redshaw)

227 <u>Charles F Worth</u> who founded his own business the "House of Worth" in Paris in 1858. An innovative and highly successful coutourier he dictated the high fashions of the Second Empire, dressing the nobility and Royal families of Europe. He introduced collections, fashions shows and the bustle. A very wealthy man he was given the Légion d' Honneur. In 1895 his state funeral was attended by the French President.

126

228 <u>A later picture of Worth's House</u> with a new front door at one side and a bay window in the centre. (compare p226)
Later known as Wake House, it became the SKDC offices but is now being renovated for use as an arts and social centre, by a voulunteer group lead by councillor Mrs. Jean Joyce.
Beyond is the Police Sation on the corner of Burghley Street. This was not a time of civil unrest in Bourne but the annual meeting of the Lincolnshire Constabulary which moved around the county!

229 North Street looking back to the Market Place with <u>the Police Station</u> on the corner of Burghley Street. Beyond are the signs of Neale's funiture shop, the Old Windmill and Six Bells. On the left is Pearson's electricians and beyond the pantile roof of the Tudor Cinema.

230 <u>A waggonload of faggots from Bourne woods,</u> often used to lay in the bottom of ditches to keep them draining, even when silted up. The dormer windowed cottage and Kelham's shop were demolished for the building of the Tudor Cinema.

231 <u>The Tudor Cinema</u> in June 1986. Opened in December 1929, it became a Bingo Hall in 1972, then in 1989, it became the Chinese restaurant of today. One can see on the gable end of Gilbert and Company's shop where the earlier cottage roof abutted. All the shops have changed hands in recent years.

232 <u>A flash flood in North Street</u> in August 1912. The spectators are gathered outside the police station on the corner of Burghley Street.

233 Probably another picture of <u>the same flood</u> a little further north outside the railings of the National School (R). I last recall a flood here in November 1968.

234 <u>The National School and Vestry Hall</u> became a Red Cross Hospital for wounded soldiers from December 1914 . The National School was built as a Sunday School in 1839. After the war it was the Red cross headquarters in the town, then it was leased as the domestic science department of the secondary school. Later sold for a gym, then bought by the Bourne and Stamford Conservative Club, they are now vacating.

235 Some <u>convalescent wounded with their Red Cross nurses</u> outside the National School during the first World War.

236 <u>The Vestry Hall</u> became part of the Red Cross Hospital in the first World War. Later sold to the BUC, it was let to the Badminton club for some years, but is now sold again.

237 <u>Inside the National School when used as the Red Cross Hospital</u> in the first World War.

238 <u>The Butterfield cottage Hospital</u>, North Road as originally given to the town by the Butterfield family in 1910, with £50 per year towards running costs. After a trial period of 3 years, it was handed over with a lump sum of £1000, but otherwise depended on fundraising.

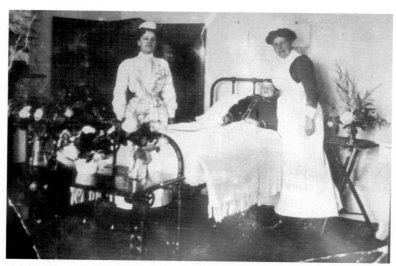

239 <u>The Butterfield's first patient</u> William Thorton, aged 5, who had fallen off Wilson's bridge down Eastgate, breaking his leg, which was set on a kitchen table. He died in July 1969 aged 63.

240 <u>The extensions to the Butterfield added as a memorial</u> to the dead of the first World War, was opened in 1921. It had two five bedded wards, male above and female below and one single room, between the top ward and the operating theatre in the nearside first floor room of the old house. The other rooms in the house provided office and flat for matron. There was a wooden extension at the rear for out patients.

241 <u>Harrington Street corner</u> with the Butterfield Hospital behind the tree and the Peterborogh Cooperative Society's shop and Pattison's tailors shop on the opposite corner.
(Ashby Swift)

242 On 20 Nov. 1924 there was a <u>fire in Kisby's grocers shop</u> on the corner of Harrington Street, which spread into Pattison's tailors shop. He was not insured so bank-rupted, although he continued tailoring for some time in the Angel long room. He was also the Town's bandmaster.

243 The rebuilt grocer's shop became <u>Woolf's car parts and accessories shop</u> with petrol pumps. I suspect the pumps were here until the garage was built across the road, now the 24hr Esso station.

244 Looking up <u>North Road from the Harrington Street turning</u> (R). Rutland Cottage of 1901 is on the left, with the picturesque thatched Cuckoo Bush cottage next. This has gone to permit the Christopher's Lane access to Digby Court, the old folks complex. Note the massive double telgraph poles, now underground with single distribution poles.

(posted 18th Sept 1914).

245 Furthur up <u>North Road before the first World War</u> as one can see the sails of Wherry's mill in the distance. The second house on the right, with bay windows on both floors, is now Chevington House residential home for the elderly. Next but one beyond is Dr Galletly's house from which the practice moved to the Health Centre in 1971, but returned here in 1998.

246 <u>Wherry's Mill on Mill Drove</u> before 1915 when it was struck by lightening and had to be reduced to two storeys. The miller Mr Barnatt is seen with three millwrights and the stones out of the building for renovation.

247 <u>North Road looking back towards the town</u> with Wherry's mill on the left and the toll gate across the road. This was in place from 1756 to 1882. (Redshaw)

248 The Tollkeeper's house on North Road (west side). The bill board on the house displays the tariff for different classes of road user e.g. 6d for a pony and trap. The message on the gate exhorts travellers to "take a ticket to Graby bar", another toll point to the north.

249 Wherry's Mill stump and adjacent sheds used by Tom Jones to store and display antiques. The same view as in picture 247, but taken on 12th February 1978. The stump was cleared away in June 1994 and the site used for house building, as was the field this side, shortly before.   (McG)

250 The hut in Little Pepper Harrow Field, at the rear of Frogmore Cottage, 105 North Road, provided by Trevor and Sheila Brodrick as the regular meeting place of the Girl Guides, until the opening of the Shippon Barn in 1977. Sheila Brodrick was a Vice President of the Lincolnshire South Girl Guides. The house on the left, behind would be Mr Ward's, 103 North Road, which looks directly across the A15 down Mill Drove.

(McG July 1967)

251 This secluded and sheltered field continued as a treasured county camp site for Guides until Trevor's death. By this time he had inherited the title of Lord Midleton and Baron Brodrick of Frogmore, so the site which is now built upon is called Midleton Gardens.

(McG July 1980)

138

252 Bourne Girl Guides in Brodrick's field for the celebration of 75 years of the Girl Guides movement in June 1985. The guiders are Mrs Margaret McGregor, County Camp advisor and Mrs Julie Maxfield.

(Lincs. Free Press)

253 Enrolment evening in Shippon Barn for the First Rainbow Unit in this area, the first year of Rainbow Guides nationally. The Guider is Mrs Susan Bellamy.

(McG 10 Oct 1988)

254 The official <u>opening of the Shippon Barn for Guides and Scouts</u> on 19 June 1977. L-R. Mr R Penny, chairman of the Premises Committee, Guide Laura Caves, Brownie Goodale, Scout John McGregor, Cub Kevin Warn and Dr M McGregor, chairman of Bourne United Charities.

(Stamford Mercury)

Which nearly brings us back to where I began –

255 Sunset over <u>St Peter's Pool</u>.

(McG 14 Jan 1994)

Apologies, Acknowledgements and Dedication

Coming to Bourne in 1961 to join Dr George Holloway in his Brook Lodge practice, it was not until the mid 1970s that I learned to copy postcards and other photographs combining my interest in photography and local history. When I started showing some of my slides to local groups, many people lent me their old photographs to copy, which I do with a hand held camera. Although I have a sizeable collection of slides I have few original prints, so inevitably there is some loss of definition, working from my copied transparencies.

For some time both JD Birkbeck's scholarly "History of Bourne" and Steve Bayliss' fascinating booklet of "Photographic Reminiscences" have been out of print. I have felt there was a place for something between these two. A collection of old photographs like the latter, but with greater annotation to add historical interest, without aspiring to be a full history.

Last year Peter Putterill, Graham Luesby and I tried to add to the Civic Society's collection of prints by re-borrowing but it proved to be too difficult to keep together both ourselves and the photographs to be able to make a fair selection.

I have now attempted a selection of my slides, which seem to have most historical interest, even some rather old and faded, adding information I have gathered from others over the years. Not being a historian myself I am most indebted to Mr Birkbeck's book, Robert Penhey, local historian and the many, some now gone, who kindly, gave me information. With no thought of publication, I recorded what little information came with the picture, but not the source of the loan. This makes re-borrowing difficult and listing my sources incomplete. So I have not attempted a list but dedicate the book to all those who have generously supplied pictures or information, and I acknowledge my great debt to them.

Nor would this have come to publication without the sustained encouragement of my wife Margaret and of the Taylor family. James Taylor, a pupil at Bourne Grammar School, has done a superb job transferring the pictures and my illegible scribblings onto computer disc, from which Warners have worked! My most grateful thanks to them all.

Any profit from the sale of this booklet will go toward Bourne Civic Society's heritage centre in Baldock's Mill.

January 2000

Apologies, Acknowledgements, and Dedication